# How to wear a skin

Louisa Adjoa Parker

Indigo Dreams Publishing

First Edition: How to wear a skin
First published in Great Britain in 2019 by:
Indigo Dreams Publishing
24, Forest Houses
Halwill
Beaworthy
Devon
EX21 5UU

www.indigodreams.co.uk



ISBN 978-1-910834-98-5

British Library Cataloguing in Publication Data. A CIP record for this book can be obtained from the British Library.



Designed and typeset in Palatino Linotype by Indigo Dreams.
Cover artwork by Jennifer Ho. www.jenniferho.co.uk.
Author photo by Robert Golden.
Printed and bound in Great Britain by 4edge Ltd.
www.4edge.co.uk

Papers used by Indigo Dreams are recyclable products made from wood grown in sustainable forests following the guidance of the Forest Stewardship Council.

for Maya and Leila

**Also by Louisa Adjoa Parker:**

*Salt-sweat and Tears*, Cinnamon Press, 2007
*Blinking in the Light*, Cinnamon Press, 2016
*1944 We Were Here: African American GIs in Dorset*, Lulu, 2014
*Dorset's Hidden Histories*, Development Education in Dorset, 2007

**CONTENTS**

# How to wear a skin

**Sunflower**
*for Melissa*

Some family do not share your blood.
I've often thought this, but on this sun-baked
morning in a Devon town I call my home, it's known.
I've woken in a house I used to sleep in

thirty years ago – the sitting room with yellow
walls, skirting licked with moss-green paint.
The bath's moved closer to the door,
as though it's trying to escape. Round paper

lampshades hang from ceilings, as they
always have. The skin under my friend's eyes
is white and, although she's tired, she's beautiful
in coral dress and Birkenstocks. Her mum's

thin as a bird; hasn't felt like eating since
her husband died. Her spine bends
towards the earth, her feet and toes are purple.
In my friend's old bedroom I remember

how us girls would sleep through mornings
in this room, which was yellow as a sunflower then,
and I understand that though life is like the river Dart –
cold water flowing seawards, its twists and turns,

the way it swells and shrinks, sometimes threatens
to erode you – and most things change,
for now, on this August morning,
some things have stayed the same.

**Beach Huts**

Next to bone-white huts
in the half-dark, where red and green lights

strung like necklaces, hang
against the sky, I want to tell the woman

with the little boy who trails behind her,
while she calls out *Charlie*

every now and then as though the word
will reach out, wrap itself around him

like rope; pull him close, I want to say
*I lived here once, I lived here, me.*

**Boy at the Station**

His arm's stiffened by a plaster cast from wrist to elbow,
an empty sleeve hangs from his shoulder, flapping

like a one-winged bird. He strides through station,
all long, thin legs in skinny jeans, Michael Jackson dancing shoes,

white tee and biker's jacket. A cigarette's stuck to his lip,
his black hair's damp with product. He loves the Fifties, films

in black and white – especially French – all the world's a film
and he's the star. Subtitles dance beneath him as he pauses

on the bridge, skitters down the iron steps with Ali-shuffling feet.
Soon he'll leave all this behind – this dead-end market town

where nothing ever happens, long weekends in 'Spoons,
the house he lives in with his mum, beige bricks and double glazing,

artexed ceilings, the constant threat of tears, her posters
of James Dean. He'll move to Paris, hole up in a loft in the city where

he'll meet his girl, all white walls and floorboards, exposed brick –
an easel he can fill with colour. He'll work as an artist;

she will be his muse – he'll use broad strokes to capture shades
in the burnt-toffee hair he loves sweeping from her neck, her clear

brown eyes, magnolia skin with just a hint of peach, the cello
curves of waist and hips, her rose-tipped breasts. They'll fling

the shutters open when it rains, breathe in wet earth, drink bottles
of red wine, fuck for days with tangled sheets entwining them.

They'll venture out for *pain au chocolat*, drink thick coffee
from shot-size cups. They'll barely eat; they'll be so full of love

there'll be no need. They'll live like every moment's a still
from some old film; the composition perfect, camera panning in

on lips, or skin on skin, zooming out to show them walking
through the dark on wet-shined cobblestones, holding hands

and laughing as he swings her arm into the air. One day
he'll bring her home, show her fields of cows with heads bent

to the grass, ducks on the river Frome, the Wednesday market
full of tat. He'll take her for a pint in 'Spoons. The two of them

will stride through this town, macs flapping in the wind
like wings. He'll show them all his one true love, how he's made

something of himself. She'll say everything is *pittoresque;*
he'll carry their suitcases with his two good arms.

**My Grandmother at Greenham Common**

Her silver-white hair stands out
bright as a naked light-bulb
amongst the women with long brown
curls and rainbow dungarees.
She tells me she can't find
a good hairdresser for miles; it's starting
to get out of control. She's wearing
her best Marks and Spencers' suit,
creased and splattered with mud. Lippy
as always, carefully applied.
A woman with a baby on her hip
says Phil is fighting to protect us.
Her eyes shine as she strokes
my Gran's arm. Nanny talks
of nuclear disarmament. She doesn't mention
Sunday roasts, or teas, or whether the tops
of her doors are dust-free. There are no cans
of Mr Sheen, but she does reach
into her tailored jacket, pulls out a nice piece
of fruitcake for me. I need feeding up –
*I'm tall, not fat.* Here, she's not beholden
to any man – free to be herself,
unafraid of what life might throw
at her. Black men don't lurk in shadows, waiting
to marry her only daughter. Her nerves
haven't got the better of her.

**What I Have Lost**

School holidays in Ghana
complaining of the heat
being spoilt by uncles
grandparents, my aunt
being *part* of something
being loved by many people
living with two cultures
side by side like twins
who are completely different
funerals and weddings
learning how to dance
knowing that I'm not
*a half-caste freak*
but someone who is more
than just one thing –
a bit of this, a bit of that.

**Duffel Coat**

He always drove the low-bottomed
red Citroen too fast; flying across
the Devon countryside
as though on a magic carpet.
Back home, he'd inch up the drive,
park on top of an old well
in his garage floor. The kitchen
always smelt of cumin.
There was a grand piano in the drawing room,
heavy velvet curtains hung
from French windows, thick with dust.
He loved talking; loved people,
loved parties. Friends would stay for weeks,
for months, for years. Sometimes
he lived in a different world to us,
even then, he tried to draw us in.
Talked of conspiracy theories, the *Greens*.
His face – like a child's, big-eyed,
wide-smiled – was framed
with a tangle of wild black hair.
Sometimes he'd fly into a rage.
He often talked of his children;
perhaps for him they didn't grow,
but stayed as tiny faces staring from a frame.
He'd lie on the chaise-longue
surrounded by piles of paper
and mustard-coloured walls.
Lit his fire with a Bunsen burner.
He didn't do housework but liked to cut the lawn.
Loved reading. Charmed women.
Outside, rotten grapes hung from a vine.
Sometimes, he'd wear his duffel coat for days.

**Butterfly**

It was the way you snapped
*Shut up,* your words cutting into mine,
your voice like my mother's, an echo
from the past. You are a self-pinned butterfly
fluttering your wings. I sit alone upstairs,
waiting for my anger to subside, thinking
*I cannot do this anymore,*
while you lean against the bar
and smoke your shisha pipe,
lament the wrongs done to you
like a film star surrounded by her fans
starved-thin, in white dress and five-inch heels
a slash of lipstick
like a cut across your face.

**I Remember Tasting Salt**

Outside the sky is pale
as the peeling white paint
on wooden-slatted walls
inside the beach hut.
Then, the warm press
of his hand on my head.
I'm not sure if I want this,
yet soon the spill of him
is white; a liquid salt, a sea
that fills my throat before
I spit him on the floor.
Outside, salt-waves move
up and down the sand.
White-winged seagulls circle
in the wind; people laugh
and walk along the rusty pier.

**A Stranger's Breath**

The stranger sitting behind me
on the train, who must have thought
that 9am was *time for a drink*
takes me back to a place
when every day, for you,
was a cause for celebration
or commiseration
and I'd wake each morning
to the smell of last night's whisky
sweating its way through your skin;
decaying your life, that deathly stink
that filled the room, our lives,
and ended yours.

**Bright Sparks**

They've been
wired together wrongly –
fuses blow too quickly
circuits short themselves
and their systems overload;
like robots of the future
made by robots
made by robots
in a factory where instructions
left by people
on how to make a robot's mind
have long been lost
to time and buried
under fine metallic dust.

**The Best Years of Her Life**

went up in smoke; sitting
in hazy bedrooms, dis-used sheds

watching the orange tip spark and glow
in the darkness, waiting for her turn,

heads nodding lazily to a reggae beat.
Washed down with booze

bought from dodgy pub landlords
or begged from older boys.

Sometimes they'd roll around, drunk
and stoned in the road, go home

smelling of sick, hashish and gin.
Chew gum and spray hairspray

to hide the smell. She'd take anything:
drink, drugs, boys (or men)

to lift her up, away
from the life she was living .

**Nothing Can Stop Him**

He laughs as the whiskey slips
down his throat, like a hot eel
burning a trail to his belly; he's in
the Bull, for now, playing
*I have Nothing* on the jukebox.

Later, he'll make his way to the Globe,
ask for a cider to wash the blues
he feels each day he wakes away.
He's not allowed in the Castle;
crusties aren't welcome in there –

the smell can put customers off
their snakebite and blacks – so he'll
wander down to the square, where
a dreadlocked busker squeezes out
*Scarborough Fair* through the holes

in a tin whistle, sip vodka stolen
from Gateway, hidden in dirty boxers,
offer sips to young girls. The busker
plays *Greensleeves,* badly, other drunks
shuffle, shouting, up the street.

He doesn't care if the drink kills him;
knows he will die before he's thirty,
doesn't know it will be heroin
running like mercury through his veins
that finally stops his heart one night
while *Angels of Death* plays on the stereo.

**Her Pink Lacy Thong**

The constant nagging of my children tires me,
as does them telling me I have *issues*. I like *arguing*.
What I like, my darling girls, is my daughters
doing as they are told, sometimes,

not seeing a salmon-pink, lacy thong flung
like a sweet wrapper on top
of a Barbie-pink, bling-encrusted bag,
not hearing *I'm staying out, Mum.*

What I like, is not seeing them make
the mistakes I made, super-sized.
I want to take my children back to my past,
so they can hear what real anger is:

so they can see me – kohl-eyed,
defiant, sixteen; hear my mother's voice:
*You look like a fucking whore.* Hear

how it bounces off walls like a glass, flung hard;
how it cuts into your heart
how it gives you a choice: keep handing it down
or try, keep trying, to do better.

**Yellow Sheets**

Afterwards, I swaddle you in plastic sheets;
yellow and crumpled as an old raincoat,
they will protect you from the rain. Today

is the first and last day. I will not look
at your face, tiny and still-pink,
I know it will accuse me. But I see

your little fingers, cold and stiff as icicles
in the morning air. It's better this way.
I place the only things I have to hand

in with you, to help you on your way;
my favourite shorts, hewn from faded jeans,
the hem trailing cotton strings

like mucous. The shorts he ripped
from me. The pink bag I always wore
on my back – I give these to you.

You are light in in the bag I carry
as I walk, sore and torn and bleeding,
deciding. I want someone to find you.

You weigh less than a bag of shopping,
as I lift you into the bin, leave you
suspended in a plastic womb.

**Bones: an end and a beginning**
*for Melanie Hall*

When they found her near the motorway,
she was nothing more
than a bag of bones:
a skull and pelvis, picked clean.
They wanted to tip the bin-bag
upside down, shake out every last
splinter of bone, look for her
hiding in the folds of black plastic;

wanted to fill the spaces in with her.
She had been rubbed out like a pencil drawing.
No trace of that toothy smile, not a strand
of her white-gold hair clung to the bones.
They wanted to fill the bag
with twenty years of tears
kissed from the other's cheek.

It was the end of years of waiting,
and the beginning of a lifetime
of knowing what they had waited
so long not to know.

## Pearls

*for Henrietta Lacks*

The Night Doctors will come for you,
like they came for her
when they cut through layers
of black skin to pink, fatty flesh,
picked out one of the tumours
growing inside her like pearls
on a sea-bed. They took a piece of her,
launched it into space.

How was she to know, when she lay
praying for death to take her,
that she would fight AIDS, be injected
into babies' arms? She thought she was
only good for having babies, growing tobacco
in fields, like those before her did,
wrapped in chains. She lies in an unmarked
grave, her tumours turned to pearlescent dust.
Un-thanked, she lives on. And on.

**it ends like this**

he wonders why he hadn't known
but perhaps he did
perhaps the heart of him has always known
it ends like this
him splayed out on the sidewalk like a giant fish
beached on grey sand as a ring of people
watch it flap its tail watch it drowning in the air
it ends like this him face-down on a bed of concrete
his tomb his only view of shoes and legs
listening to the voices of white men hungry for his blood
as they poke their fingers into the soft folds of his flesh
the grandsons of the men who strung
trees with his forebears as though they were lanterns
it ends like this with men pressing the breath from him
an arm wrapped around his throat
like a lover's final embrace
it ends like this him choking out the words
*I can't breathe I can't breathe I can't breathe*

## Burma

After the rains
the dead float, belly-up;
bloated water lilies
with starfish hands
stretched skywards,
imploring their Gods
to save them.

## Breaking Point

### I Breaking

Bones break, then slowly knit
together. Skulls fold in upon
themselves when smashed. Bone china,
glass, when dropped, splits from a whole
into immeasurable pieces.
Hearts break, then mend, and break
again. News breaks in red
across our TV screens. Waves break
on our shores. Breaking – to come apart,
to split the way our country did –
into sharp-edged halves
like a plate dropped on the floor.

### II Point

A conversation has a point, or not.
The tip of a pencil, scrawled on a ballot slip
has a point until it's blunted.
Campaigns have a point, sometimes.
Or they are run by pointless fools
with bad hair days and rubber smiles
who don't expect to win, then walk away,
leave us picking up the pieces
of ourselves, littering the ground
like broken glass, watching
as they catch the light.

## Take Back Control

**I**

Take children from their mothers
wrap them in chains and brand their skin.
Take half the world and wash it pink.
Take history, take lives.
Take racism and smash it into chips.
Take gold, take spices, land.
Take food and let them starve.
Take the best bits of other people's cultures.
Take race and slice it thinly into cards.
Take truth and replace it carefully with lies.

**II**

Back to a golden age, a glorious time
of Pakistani-bashing, the stampede
of Doctor-Martened feet, shaved heads
and swastikas; of making England great again.
Back to a time of waving flags,
shouting *Go Home* to anyone who looks
as though they might be foreign.
Back to a time before political correctness
went mental, and stitched good English lips
with silence, so they had to preface
every sentence with *I'm not a racist, but…*
Back to a time before England –
like a sober friend –
laid her hand on forearms
in pubs across the land,
said with a pained smile and shake
of her head, *Bruv, not cool. Not cool at all.*

**III**

Control the borders! Build a wall
so we can keep them out. Control
the hordes, the floods, the swarms,
the waves of foreigners who wash ashore
our island. Control the welfare state!
Do not give money to the undeserving.
Control the immigrants
who run around like cockroaches
with pincer hands and dark-shined bodies
taking things that don't belong to them
– our jobs, our homes, our way
of life – to their filthy, vermin nests.

**Those wild, pre-Brexit days**
*after Josephine Corcoran*

Do you remember those wild, pre-Brexit days
when immigrants filled our seas with their bodies,
floated death onto our beaches
forced us to see images of dead immigrant children
while we were eating our cereal and drinking our tea?

And a man couldn't take a shit in his own toilet
without finding an immigrant squatting over the bowl
and when he went to work the immigrants had run off with his job.
And when immigrants crawled out of gutters
and when immigrants crawled out of the seas.

Do you remember those wild, pre-Brexit days
when the immigrants killed our language
how when a man walked down his own street,
it was like living in Syria, or Poland or some godforsaken place,
and a man had to listen to them chattering like monkeys

and when he went to the corner shop
the immigrants had bought all the white sliced
and immigrants owned the shop, too!
And when he went to the job centre they'd run off with his benefits.
And when immigrants crawled out of gutters
and when immigrants crawled out of the seas.

Do you remember those wild, pre-Brexit days
when immigrants stole all our women
and when a man tried to make love to his own wife
an immigrant had climbed into his bed,
slid between his cotton sheets
and was running his immigrant hands

all over her English rose skin
and a man had to watch while the immigrant took her –
while he whispered sweet nothings in *foreign*!
And when a man went downstairs to make tea
an immigrant poured himself out of the kettle.

And immigrants crawled out of the gutters.
And immigrants crawled out of the seas.

**The town that I ran to to keep me safe**

The town that I ran to, to dodge somebody's fists.
The town that I ran to like a child
seeking shelter under a tree during a storm.
The town where I have made mistakes
and no-one forgets, but they might forgive,

where for some I'll always be
*that black woman*
with different fathers for her kids.
The town where I've grown up, along with my kids.
The town I thought was pretty with the sea wall

curling round the harbour like an ammonite.
The town where you can stand at the school gates
and feel like a stranger after ten years, where
mothers stand in batches, hatch gossip
like battery hens laying eggs.

The town where my daughter's family pass her
blankly, on the street. The town
that holds pain in its pockets like drops
of mercury, where I have buried men,
where stories unfold against a backdrop of bird cries.

**His Khaki Hood**

A woman with a baby
in a backpack stops me
in the street when it's just
begun to rain and hail
and the sky is bright
the way a child's eyes
glitter darkly when
they are about to cry. She says
*Excuse me, can you put his hood up?*
So I lift the hood of her
baby's khaki coat, gently
around his head; I love
this woman for not being afraid
to stop a stranger in the street
and ask for help keeping
her little boy's head dry in the rain.

**Somehow, she knows just what to do**

picks up the ink-blue doll
which has replaced her child, blows life back in.

Old memories of first-aid classes come back;
she brings her daughter back from death, stops

her slipping into the space between sounds.
She thinks fresh air will help; runs barefoot

over cobblestones in the heat-baked yard
holds her daughter up to the sky – not offering her

to the Gods, but begging her to stay. *Come back,*
she shouts, *Mummy loves you.*

After the hospital: they take turns to watch her
day and night, sleep-starved but grateful,

watching to make sure her tiny belly
will not stop rising up and down.

**Smiling Mummies**

Today, when I am minding being alone,
I cannot face the hordes of tourists: smiling
Mummies using the 'D' word to their kids –

*Daddy will get the fish and chips –*
cheerful Daddies giving shoulder rides
and loving their children, and not being dead.

Prickly-eyed, I turn and walk another way;
what I need is solitude and the stink
of seaweed, brown ribbons shining in heaps;

what I need is the shush-shush sound of waves.
What I need, is to turn the corner, and not see
a pair of rainbow-collared pigeons, kissing.

**The Scarlet Ladies Come To Town**

Scarlet ladies in crinolines the colour
of fresh blood swirl and twirl their skirts;

heady with excitement, feverish, rose-cheeked,
they charm my daughters into letting them in.

At night the scarlet ladies paint their redness
on my children's faces, turn their tongues

to strawberries, swell their throats and glands.
Then they go out and paint the town red, laughing.

I wish the scarlet ladies would go, leaving
nothing behind but their red and white hankies

and the faint smell of their fever.
I shake my fists at the scarlet ladies,

when no-one is looking. For days, I hydrate dry lips
and cool burning throats, place bowls of hot water

in rooms, open and shut windows, wet flannels.
The scarlet ladies have lips the colour of post-boxes.

I see them watching me, out of the corner of my eye.
I think of children centuries ago, convalescing,

left delicate, pale-faced. I think of heroines in novels
with weak constitutions. I think of my daughters

being carried off by the ladies in red. I ask the doctor
*Is it fatal*? She laughs, *It looks terrible, keep doing*

*what you're doing, well done.* Scarlatina.
It's party time for the scarlet ladies, twirling

their silky fresh-blood skirts, smiling
their silly smiles, setting my daughters on fire.

## Fruit Machine

I want to bang my head
against a wall until
the *right answer* falls out of me
lands at my feet
like a coin
from a fruit machine.

**Red Stripe**

She arrives
with a big suitcase
a rounded belly,
a new boyfriend.
He greets me
with *Hello, Nan.*
She leaves emptied.
All that is left
of him: a photo
of her belly,
a red stripe
in a white toilet bowl.

## Bread and Rubies

they say
the first cut is the deepest
daughter, you may as well
have scored a line
across my heart as your own arm

was it the first? will it be the last
or a taste of more to come?
how did it feel, your pale flesh parted
crimson drops of life-blood
like a row of rubies on just-fallen snow?

i pick up a knife in my kitchen
slice through fresh bread
the crumbs scattered on the worktop
are white and soft as your skin

**In the A&E Car Park**

let him not be lost
let him not slip away
let him not become
a figment of our imaginations
running around on sturdy legs
let him stay
let him play football in the park
let him eat ice cream
let him see trees, dappled with light
let him stay
let him not be lost
let him not slip away

**Boiling Kettles**

An endless loop of panic:
will the house burn down
while I'm away? Will it still
be standing when I return?
*Will* I return? Are the hair straighteners
unplugged, the cooker turned off?
Will water pipes freeze and burst?
Will burglars get in?
I think of ghosts of irons
flat-down on burning boards
of kettles boiling, on repeat.

## Seeing The World The Right Way Up

She flies in this summer, her smooth face
unchanged as always;
brings her daughter, grown tall,
suitcases and her way of seeing
my life which is different to mine.
*The best thing you ever did was stay*
*and bring your girls up here.*
She left back then, in search
of bright lights, black
nameless faces, dirty glamour, shapes
like her own, where she would slip
into the crowd like silk.
She'd been drawn to us
by our gold-brown skin,
which lit us like beacons in this town
where white faces swam every day
in front of our brown ones, stared open-mouthed
like fish watching other fish
in their glass bowls.
Now, fifteen years on, she spells it out
as though arranging
coloured letters on my fridge door:
*Look. Where You Live.*
I think of her in London; in that fraction of time
she turns my world the right way up.

## Black Orchid

The folds of silk are white as a moon;
my ebony skin is the night sky.
Women glide around the room like swans,
dipping long white necks, waiting
for a man to pull them into an embrace,
murmur *You are beautiful* in their ears.
I stand alone, fanning cool air
across my face, my breasts,
while chandeliers drip jewels
like hailstones suspended above our heads.
He comes, whispers to me
in the dark heat of the night.
I am a black orchid, rare in my beauty.

I will never know the little white girl,
born free, with gold hoops in her ears,
to a mother who thinks more of the men
who beat her than her own child, a girl
who sits on buses as black folk nod
at her thick lips, familiar nose, green
eyes with flecks of hazel, the little white girl
who smooths her hair flat against her head
nods to beats in bars, lets men take her
like they took her mother:
the girl who will never know
that her grandmother's grandmother's
grandmother once held moon-bright silk
against the night of her skin.

**One Girl**
*after Helen Frame*

Her skin is butterscotch Angel Delight
And her hair a nest of spun burnt sugar
And her eyes espresso shots and her *best feature*
And she's free as a gull in the sky
And she's seventeen like festivals in Cornwall
And smoke-filled tents and mud and *E*s
And she's sad like George Michael on the radio
at Christmas and Snoopy's ears and her mum's eyes
And she's come through adolescence like a big dipper
And she's tired like old slippers
and scared like Freddy Krueger's fingers
And she loves like her heart's made of steel
And her face is a harvest moon in a navy sky
And she's wild like gorse on the moors
And delicate as spider-webs at dawn
Her hands want other hands to hold them
And her lips are big like goldfish
And her legs are lumps of clay
And nothing like a model's
And her belly's soft like kisses
And her heart is blue blown glass

And one man
like a black-eyed starling
digging for worms in the dawn

## Girls in High Heels

They clip-clop past like horses,
heels raised high, their bodies tipped
towards the night, dresses tight

as a second skin. Their shoes pinch and rub,
but tomorrow's blisters – angry buttons
of skin – are worth it. Their feet are bound

by bone-hard leather that does not flex
or breathe; these shoes are made to crush feet
not caress them. Spines thrust forwards,

they trot towards the bar, a beacon
in the night, full of men who will tell them
they are beautiful. They'll spend

half a month's wages on heels to line up
in their wardrobes like a parade. At the end
of the night, drunk, with aching feet,

they'll take their shoes off, step barefoot
around dog-shit, condoms, broken glass,
shoes like baubles dangling from their hands.

**Beautiful**

She could be thought pretty, albeit
in an exotic, far-flung-lands way.
Life was what she made it;
not easy to navigate its winding roads.
Blue days or gold days, she wouldn't
let it beat her down. Sometimes
she remembered the flat of his hand
against her skin. She wasn't built for this.
She dreamed of running free
and wild, floating like a falling leaf
through her days, telling her tale.

## Woman, Stripped Bare

It is late. I watch
as he makes a journey
inches but hours long.
This is animal,
it's a she-wolf, crouched
in her lair, snarling.
It's a stripping back
of womanhood, a peeling
of dignity to reveal pink flesh,
bright blood and screams.
Out there, cities are crumbling
to make way for him. White
cherry blossom trees are bursting
into flower. With a new day, new light,
there comes new life.

## Moonlight

I feel the cold press of wood
on the nape of my neck as I lean
against the window frame.
Our breathing finds a rhythm
in the still night; his quick,
child-sweet breaths, mine
slower, bitter with years.
He's curled against my chest,
damp with sleep, grateful for the sight
of fields, the glow of street-lamps,
the night-shadows of trees
which stop his cries.
The perfect curve of his cheek
is a white crescent in the darkness
as he drifts in and out of sleep,
breathes in moonlight like air.

## The Most Beautiful Girl in the World

*for Maya*

She arrives into the world at her own pace
like a girl late for her own party
the cord wrapped – twice! – loosely
round her neck as if it were a feather boa,
or flower garland – *Doesn't it suit me?*
Not knowing this will terrify her nana
with *what ifs* for days.

Propelled through lukewarm water,
she doesn't cry. With dark, wide-open eyes
she looks at her mum, at her dad,
back to Mum again – there's no surprise,
only cool recognition
as if she was expecting them,
as if she's been here in the world all along.

**Cream and Roses**

She doesn't look like me.
There's little trace of the *exotic*
in her cream-and-roses skin
her pale, kink-less hair, smooth
as a bolt of silk. Although,
like her mother,
her forehead browns easily
in the sun. She may not look
like me, yet she has my arch-less
feet, my love of sugar, of books,
of people, love of life. She has
my blood, my history,
my love. She fits
so neatly in my heart.

## Kite

It's early. Her feet on
fallen leaves crunch
like a child eating dry cornflakes
from a bowl. She moves
closer to the gate; slats of wood
gape like broken teeth.
There is a hawk – dead,
wet-feathered, grey:
a fallen kite in a stream.
Its yellow claw curled like a hand
trying to hold the last seconds
of life. Death came quickly.
Somewhere, a cockerel crows.
Clear water flows over stones.

**Dancing With Atoms**

Although he has shrunk
to nothing but a quiet voice
whispered through a microphone
and we strain to catch the words
like children trying to catch
raindrops on their tongues,
he still has so much to say;
finds the words, squeezes them
through his lips like final breaths.

Although his body is still,
has wound down like a broken clock,
his mind can't stop moving; rises up
of his body, the bed he has lain in
for years, this flat, this town
by the sea; his mind soars into the sky,
out into the universe, dances with atoms
and theories and stardust
travels through time, across
continents, feels hot sun again,
sees mountains topped with snow.

**Thirteen**

You're just thirteen, with Mum-cropped 'Fro.
You love sweets, riding your BMX. You're beginning
to love boys. You cry, but refuse to see him in his coffin.
Later, you're not sure if you even said the words,
*My Granddad's died*. The house bleeds too many tears
from its walls; you're still a girl – life is to be lived,
first cigarettes to be smoked, friends to be made
and lost, lips to be kissed. You don't know then that grief
can tuck itself inside you, take years to work its way
up to the surface of your skin. You don't know
that mid-forties, you'll remember the scratch
of his moustache, his brycleemed hair. His smile.
The way he'd say *Would you like a mint, Christine,*
to your mum, knowing how she hated them.
You'll imagine faint smells of cigarettes and Sunday roasts.
You'll dream he's here and wake to find he's gone.
You'll think of him, how his knees buckled as he fell,
how the last thing he'd have seen was the hard, bright shine
of the toilet bowl your grandmother kept so clean.

**Love, Ending**

Love ends how it begins.
The suddenness startles you
like the wingtips of a late-home bird
brushing your cheek in the dark.

Love, when it comes, spills across,
fills your world like rising seas.
Now it has gone, there is no bright star
out there, loving you, carrying
your heart in theirs.

Like tides, love quickly retracts
– cold water moving over stones.
Whereas once it flooded you,
now the shore is empty
and in the quiet, seagulls cry a name.

**I'll Still Be Me Without You**

I'll still be me without you,<br>
the world won't stop.<br>
Ceilings won't fall in, houses<br>
won't crumble to dust, flowers<br>
won't bend their petalled heads and curl<br>
back into the earth, blackberries<br>
won't rot overnight. Sheep won't roll<br>
over dead in their fields like unwanted<br>
balls of wool, cars won't stop in the roads,<br>
the earth won't forget to move round the sun,<br>
the sea won't fail to tide, lights won't flicker<br>
then fade, windows won't shatter, no-one<br>
will scream – the world won't stop.<br>
I'll still be me without you, you'll still be you, the world<br>
will dance on.

## Unclaimed

She wears her lover's name inked
into the pale skin above a nub of spine –

*Dean* in curling letters, ink blue as jays,
in old font, as though a scholar

from antique days dipped a quill
into his well, scratched words into her skin.

Her hair is pinned into a bun, exposing
the soft nape of her neck, black grips criss-cross

through her hair. Her mates – all knee-slashed jeans
and Nike trainers – told her, *You'll regret it*

*when you're old,* faces scrunched into concern,
heads cocked, like a row of tiny birds.

But she, sixteen, belief in him stretching
from the roots of her, knew their love

would never fade or fall right off the page.
She bore the tattooist's needles bravely,

head dipped low, chin resting on her chest.
*It was my idea,* she'd say, and blush,

remembering how he'd swept his hand
over that piece of unmarked skin, say, *A tat*

*would look good here, babe,* as though it was a patch
of unclaimed, scrubby earth he had plans to develop.

No matter how she'd twist her neck, or use two mirrors,
she couldn't see it fully. Dean took photos on his phone

when the scabs fell from her skin, revealing how
she was marked as his – an inky love-bite, swirled in blue.

He'd kiss the letters, as though it was himself
he loved, not her. One day, other men will pull elastic

from her bun, watch hair fall to her shoulders,
suggest she wears her hair unpinned.

**On Waking**

As I blink the night away I hear
clear notes of falling rain –

a single, steady drip onto the roof,
the thrum of drops falling together

like fingers on a drum. A seagull's
keening cry. The window's etched

with leaves like frost flowers
on a winter morning, slashed

with elongated drops of rain.
Through the glass I see the shadow

of scaffolding – a metal skeleton
rearing at the sky, filtering the light

like passing clouds. I open the window,
smell wet earth and rain, stare at rusty poles

and wooden boards splashed
with orange paint. Soon the builders

will be here, all shouts and drills
and bangs. I'll have to fight

the urge to shout, *Be quiet*! I pull
the window shut, let the morning come.

**Warm Pebbles**

I have decided he will make a considerate lover.
He is as attentive as someone tracking butterflies.
I think of him treating my body the same way.
All week, I have been remembering his hands

on my waist; desire moving through me
like a slow-worm wriggling in the heat.

Now, I consider briefly, deciding we *can*
become lovers. Then we plunge headfirst, swimmers
in a Christmas sea. He places kisses like warm pebbles
in the small of my back. Afterwards, I can feel them there for days.

**i want to taste your smile**

like a low-slung sun suspended over rooftops in a sky the colour of oranges i want to feel your hands on my hips your lips against mine whispering *you are beautiful* kissing the top of my head i want to lie with you with windows flung open and the rain coming in i want to share the stars with you share the moon with you the sea the night i want to lie in parks all day breathing in strangers the sounds of traffic with the sun getting hotter on our backs i want to walk on beaches getting stones in my shoes i want you to hold me stroke me like water want to wake to your smile

like the sun

## She wants to dance at night

as the sun goes down, a gold
dress clinging to her rounded hips
– hips which are beautiful here –
skin blackened by the sun;
she wants to dance to a different beat,
dance till the sweat on her skin grows cold,
dance till her limbs ache, dance
to stories drummed out in beats,
dance to the sounds of lovers
this hot night, wrapped only in sheets,
dance to the sound of crickets.
She wants to dance under a different sky,
bright beads at her throat,
flowers in her hair, barefoot in the sand,
until the sun comes up once more.

**The Blueness of the Sky Has Changed**

So this is how it ends: an open window,
sunlight, birdsong, the sounds
of children playing.  Curtains blowing
in the breeze. A husk – the shape of him –
under a white sheet. His open mouth,

the liquid rattle of his lungs.
Through the window: the oily shine
of a blackbird's feather on the grass,
flowers coming into bloom too late.

It changes everything: the blueness of sky,
heat of the sun. Each time, a clean,
bright shock. And this: But where *is* he?
Where has he gone?

## Land, Real and Imagined

Yes, I am from here, *really*,
but also from there. My feet
connect me to this piece of earth
which rolls away in green waves,

this piece of earth inhabited
by people who do not look like me.
This is how I wear my skin:
it tells the story of another place;

an imagined country
with dusty roads, hot nights,
which I have yet to see.
We all lean into the dark

towards our ancestors, who lean
towards us, with bent spines,
trying to tell us where we are from,
where we are going.

## Sky

While the surgeons with long fingers
are opening up his rib cage
as though he is a tin of beans
and his heart is something good to eat;
while the clear-eyed surgeons
like angels in blue scrubs
try to fix my father's breaking heart,
I lie on grass that's strewn with daisies
stare skywards through cupped fingers,
red leaves pressed against the sky
and my heart aches in my ribs.

## How To Be A Good Daughter

Forgive him. Wholly and completely
even though last week you'd decided
it was better not to see him. Dig deep
into the chambers of your heart.
Do not forgive, then un-forgive, and then
forgive again. Understand
he is a person too. Accept
he isn't like you – you cannot see
his heart beat under the surface
of his skin. Forget the past,
forget the man who planted fear
which grew and flowered in you.
See instead the thin old man
in front of you, with whitened hair,
his glasses perched halfway down his nose.
Cry when your sister tells you
he keeps a photo of you all as children
on his mantelpiece. Cry after you get the call
when he says, *Love you,* at the end.
Pack your things and go to him.
Stare at the black-oil shine
of the blackbird hopping on the railway.
Breathe air and light into your heart.
Lift up your chin, and smile.

**An Afternoon in August**
*for Jemima*

Although it's August, the blackberries are ripening
early, so we load the children into the red wagon

with a plastic pint glass each to collect the berries.
We can't find any in the bramble bushes bordering the park

like a lace hem, but my friend finds some in an alley, hiding
under clematis. We reach for the higher ones; the children pick

the ones low down. There is peace to be found in foraging
for food, the way berries burst, bright juice staining

your skin. The baby sits in the wagon smiling like a tiny king,
a parrot hat for his crown, juice staining his face, as he dips

his hand in and out of the cup – as though the berries are purple
jewels, or spun of finest gold – saying *Thank you, more*. The boys eat

as we pick. My girl saves hers so she can share them with her mum.
Back home we sit outside, the children play in the summerhouse

with its French-grey walls, each strip of decking painted
in a different colour. Boy's clothes strung against the sky –

checked shirts, pyjama bottoms with blue stars dancing
over them. My friend sits at her garden table, face

scrubbed clean and bare of make-up, chopping vegetables,
talking, while the boys sneak pieces of courgette.

Above our heads a green triangle hangs suspended in the sky,
like a frozen kite. It's called a garden sail, as though this quiet,

happy space – all plants and colour, light-dappled wood,
children who are kept close by – is a ship this family sails on.

**Acknowledgements**

Acknowledgements are due to the editors of the following publications, in which some of the poems, or earlier versions of them, appeared: The Colverstone Review, Wasafiri, Envoi, Under the Radar, Bare Fiction, Irisi, Ouroboros Review, And Other Poems, Live Canon Anthology 2016, Wildsound, Out of Bounds (Bloodaxe), Ink, Sweat and Tears, Writing Motherhood (Seren), Disability Arts Online, The Colour of Madness (Stirling Publishing), The Big Issue, Alliterati, and In search of sea glass (Headlight Press). 'Yellow Sheets' was shortlisted by the Bridport Prize; 'Bones: an end and a beginning' was highly commended by the Abergavenny Competition in the form of a prose piece called 'Bin Bag'; 'Breaking Point' was shortlisted by the Live Canon International Poetry Prize and, along with 'Those wild, pre-Brexit days' and 'Take Back Control,' was written and performed as part of a collaboration with Josephine Corcoran for The Enemies Project; 'Those wild pre-Brexit days' was shortlisted for the Ink, Sweat and Tears July 2018 pick of the month, and was one of their Forward Prize poetry entries.

Massive thanks go to Arts Council England for supporting this collection; Nii Ayikwei Parkes for being a fantastic guest-editor; Jan Fortune for mentoring me and supporting my early writing; all of the 30/30 National Poetry Day Challenge group for prompts and inspiration; Jennifer Ho for the beautiful cover illustration; my mum Christina Palfrey for believing I'd write one day; my husband Peter Fry for always being there; my children Keziah Bell, Jessamyn Parker and Alicia Parker, and friends for believing in me and my work.

Indigo Dreams Publishing Ltd
24, Forest Houses
Cookworthy Moor
Halwill
Beaworthy
Devon
EX21 5UU
www.indigodreams.co.uk